Asset Protection for

the Real Estate Investor

and

Other Professionals

Copyright © 2016 by Real Property Experts LLC
Published by: Real Property Experts LLC

ISBN 10: 1540765245
ISBN 13: 978-1540765246

Printed in USA

This publication is designed to provide accurate and authoritative information regarding the subject matter covered. It is sold with the understanding that the publisher is not engaged in rendering legal, accounting, or other professional advice. If legal advice or other expert assistance is required, the services of a competent professional person should be sought. (From a *Declaration of Principles* jointly adopted by a committee of the American Bar Association and a committee of publishers and associations).

Library of Congress Control Number: 2016920201
CreateSpace Independent Publishing Platform, North Charleston, SC

This book is dedicated to the

real estate investor and all professionals

who have the fortitude and dedication

to go beyond the normal

and be resolved in their professions.

Asset Protection for

the Real Estate Investor

and

Other Professionals

By Pierre Mouchette

Contents

PREFACE

The information provided in *Asset Protection for the Real Estate Investor and Other Professionals* is for illustration purposes only and in no way, represents a proposal or specific recommendations. The reader is cautioned that the information presented cannot be substituted for competent legal advice. The material covered is general and is not intended as a comprehensive representation of all relevant issues. Laws in each state will vary, and the applicability of the information provided in this book may change depending on specific circumstances.

This book is written in an easy-to-read format to help provide the reader with questions and options to review with professional advisers.

Pierre Mouchette, author

SECTION 1   A Litigious Society

1.0   Introduction

As a successful real estate investor, you become acutely aware of how visible and attractive you are for lawsuits (from the public, employees, competitors, and government). Within the pages of this book, we will provide you with various options for protecting your assets.

It has been noted that even the most frivolous lawsuit can easily reach $50,000 to $100,000 and more. When an attorney sues you, he is exploiting human nature. He knows if you have reachable and collectible assets, the risk of loss will cause you extreme worry and stress. He knows that if you choose to fight, your time and privacy will be violated, and your resources will be depleted or exhausted in needless legal fees and costs.

It is the objective of this book to help you determine (with the aid of consultation with your attorney) the most objective way of protecting your assets.

1.1   Asset Protection

A properly designed asset protection plan can protect you and your business from the "successful lawyer" who can create a clever new theory of liability so that his client can take your hard earnings. Asset protection has two basic goals: to minimize the risk of potential liability and to preserve your assets. Specific areas of concern are as follows:

A. Employees: If employees do not have a proper understanding of employment laws, sexual discrimination, and preferentialism. Employers can be held accountable for the actions of their employees.

B. Contracts: A contract is formed any time parties make an agreement to do, or not to do, something. Certain types of contracts must be in writing to be valid, but most contracts do not have to be. A promise that you make is considered a contract if the other party relies on your promise. Claims of contract based on an oral agreement are difficult to defend against.

C. Negligence: You are considered negligent if a party is injured or if property is damaged because you did not exercise reasonable care (direct negligence). You may also be sued when you are legally responsible for the wrongful acts of others (imputed negligence).

D. Information: Thanks to the Internet, your life history (business and personal) is readily available using a few keystrokes. This technology makes it easy for anyone to gather information about you. Additionally, there are several information brokers that readily provide their services for a modest fee.

1.2   Risk Insurance

There are insurance policies available to the real estate investor that will help to minimize the impact of loss from many of the investor's daily operations.

The three levels of coverage, all of which should include liability coverage are.

A. Basic: insures against loss from fire, lightning, explosion, windstorm or hail, smoke, riot or civil commotion, vandalism, and sprinkler system leakage.

B. Broad form: insures against the "basics" listed above plus losses from glass breakage, falling objects, weight of snow or ice, water damage from plumbing systems, and certain collapse.

C. Special form: insures against all losses except the exclusions listed in the policy.

Umbrella coverage is the ultimate coverage and can be a cost-effective way to significantly increase your liability protection. Working in conjunction with your primary policy, it kicks in once the primary policy limits have been exhausted.

1.3   Did You Know

The following presents a liability to you and should be isolated from other family assets:

- Your car is being driven by an elderly member of your household and is involved in an accident.

- A teenager in your family gets into an auto accident.

1.4   This Book

It is not the attempt of this book to suggest asset protection through fraudulent conveyance, but it is to suggest methodologies to protect your assets from the uncertainties of a litigious society. Additionally, this book does not go into onshore (Wyoming, Delaware, and/or Nevada) or offshore asset protection since this method of protection (legally and in compliance with the tax code) is continually changing.

SECTION 2   What Happens in a Lawsuit

2.0   The Lawsuit

A lawsuit has five separate stages:

A. Economic analysis of the case: This is where the attorney reviews the economics of the case, i.e., the cost of prosecuting, the likelihood of winning, and the amount of probable recovery.

B. The pleading: The initial pleading in a case is the "complaint," which is prepared on behalf of the plaintiff. It sets forth the allegations of the defendant's wrongdoing.

- Prejudgment Writ of Attachment: This is used to "freeze" the assets of the defendant and place them under court protection prior to a judgment. If the defendant is subject to the freezing of all assets, he or she may be forced to accept a fast and unfavorable settlement.

C. Discovery: This allows each side of the lawsuit to investigate the other side for evidence as well as legal theories that will be useful to build the case and further expose the opposing side's strategy.

- The legal team will attempt to *bury* the opponent in paperwork (interrogatories, depositions, and subpoenas).

- Medical and psychiatric evaluations may be permitted.

- Computers can be subpoenaed to search documents and emails.

D. Trial: Concerns about legal fees, costs, and which way the jury will vote are always a component in the defendant's willingness to settle a case before trial. Per the "American Rule," each party to a lawsuit is required to pay its own expenses. The exception to the American Rule is that parties to a contract may specify in the agreement that in the event of a dispute, the prevailing party is entitled to recover any costs incurred in a lawsuit, including legal fees.

E. Collection: After one party, has won a lawsuit, the case is then moved to the collection stage of the lawsuit.

- The appeal: In appealing the judgment, you would have to obtain an appeal bond through a licensed bonding company that would require you to post an asset in the amount of the judgment. The amount posted must have a greater value than the sale amount that you are posting so that the bondsman will net the posted amount. Next, the bondsman's fee (usually 10 percent) must be paid. To have the appeal heard, you must pay for trial transcripts and retain an appellate lawyer who will charge you $XXXXXX. *Wow!* As a litigant, would it have been cheaper to settle or to have avoided the lawsuit through planning?

  Note: Appeals are fine for large corporations that have the financial ability to pay for them. For the average company, the right to appeal is an illusory consolation.

- Collection process: After judgment, location of the debtor's assets becomes the focus of the investigation. The debtor's exam may be presented by written questions or by oral examination. This exam is given under oath, and the debtor is asked to list and describe all assets and provide all banking records. The debtor is also asked if any transfers of property or gifts were made prior to or during the lawsuit. The failure to provide true and complete answers is a felony.

The procedure for enforcing judgments and collections by a judgment creditor is established by the laws of each state.

F. Assets: The court issues a "writ of execution," which is the legal *go-ahead* for the marshal (or sheriff) to seize (take control of) the defendant's assets and place them in safekeeping.

Real estate: A writ of execution can be filed on your properties with the city/town (county) recorder. This results
in a lien against the real estate. After proper notice, the creditor can foreclose the lien and force the sale of the property. The property can be sold at auction to the highest bidder, with proceeds from the sale used to satisfy the judgment. If, after the sale, all obligations have been paid (including judgment, interest, and other expenses) and there are surplus funds left over, they are returned to the debtor.

Note: Properties sold at auction return "wholesale" prices (forty to fifty cents on the dollar).

- Business property: Property owned by the business is subject to seizure.

- Personal residence: Depending upon the state, homestead exemptions may protect the home.

- Bank accounts and brokerage accounts: These accounts can be seized through a writ of execution. That includes money owed to you by others.

SECTION 3   The Assessment

3.0   The Assessment

Determining what you must protect and what liabilities you may have is most likely the first step to take. To organize our thoughts, let's start with the following format: first look at yourself as a real estate investor, and then look at yourself as an individual. Use the following outline to help gather your thoughts:

A. How is my business organized to protect it against the following:

- Legal mistakes

- Financial turnarounds

- Liability and lawsuits

- Dissolution

B. How are my real estate holdings organized to prevent the following:

- Legal mistakes

- Liability and lawsuits

C. How am I personally isolated against the following:

- Company risk and liability

- Liability and lawsuits

- Nonperforming investments

- Unexpected medical expenses

3.1   The Plan

A properly designed asset protection plan will accomplish most of the outlined objectives. It will minimize potential risk of liability by creating legal barriers that insulate wealth from threats, and it will preserve personal and business assets. It will do the following:

- Reduce exposure to potential lawsuits

- Protect business assets

- Protect accounts receivable

- Protect family assets

- Protect family savings and investments from lawsuits and claims

- Eliminate probate

- Reduce estate taxes

An investment in knowledge pays the best interest.

Benjamin Franklin

SECTION 4   Probate

4.0   General

When a person dies owning property not protected by a trust, a court will supervise the transfer of that property to those people named in the decedent's will. This is accomplished under court supervision by a person designated in the will as the executor of the estate.

If the decedent dies without a will, the property passes to relatives per laws of the state where he resided, and that's handled under the court's appointed administrator.

An executor or administrator is known as a personal representative and has the responsibility to perform the following:

- Locate, inventory, and appraise all the assets of the decedent

- Make final payment to all the decedent's creditors

- Prepare and file any federal and state death tax returns

- Distribute the assets of the decedent's estate according to the decedent's will or according to state law

The personal representative will usually hire an attorney to perform this work on the representative's behalf. The attorney is paid directly from the estate for services rendered. The amount of legal fees, depending upon the state, is either a fixed percentage (2 percent to 10 percent) of the gross value of the estate or is based on what the judge determines to be a reasonable fee.

The reason most people do not want their estate to go through probate is that the process is time consuming, expensive, and inconvenient. It also causes a lot of stress and frustration for the survivors.

SECTION 5   Asset Protection Strategies

5.0   General

According to the Internal Revenue Service (IRS), there are four types of real estate taxpayers:

A. Real estate investor: This is someone who actively or passively invests in real estate. An active investor may buy a property, make repairs and/or improvements to the property, and sell it later for a profit. A passive investor might hire a real estate firm to find and manage an investment property for them.

B. Real estate dealer: This individual has a trade or business in buying, holding, and selling real estate. The real estate dealer is actively involved in the business. A dealer cannot defer gain from the sale of real estate until the dealer is in receipt of the funds. A dealer pays self-employment tax.

C. Real estate professional: This is a qualified professional who is actively involved in a real estate activity in which he or she develops, redevelops, constructs, reconstructs, acquires, converts, rents, operates, manages, leases, or sells real estate. The professional spends more time (a minimum of 750 hours per year) in real estate activity than other businesses that the professional owns. The real estate professional has at least five hundred hours of material participation in each property.

D. Real estate developer: This is someone who is engaged in real estate activities that range from the renovation and re-lease of existing buildings to the purchase of raw land and the sale of developed land or parcels to others. Real estate developers are actively involved in and coordinate all activities in converting ideas from paper to real property. Developers usually take the greatest risk in the creation or renovation of real estate.

Note: The real estate dealer/developer/investor status is determined on a property-by-property case. Generally, you will want the investor status since it avoids the self-employment tax and accelerates tax due on properties with a note of the dealer and the uniform capitalization requirements of the developer.

No matter what type of investor you are, you want to protect your investment and limit your exposure to lawsuits. Asset protection goals should include the following:

A. Minimize loss

- Limited liability company (LLC): provides asset protection as well as being a conduit for income tax treatment (no double taxation)

- Limited partnership (LP): offers pass-through tax treatment and legal protection

- Family limited partnership (FLP): offers tax savings through valuation discounts when passing wealth from older family members to younger ones

- Trademarks, patents, and copyrights

- Liability insurance

- Personal umbrella liability insurance

- Key man insurance

- Long-term care insurance

- Employee handbook

Note: For the purposes of this book, we have not included the following:

- Sole proprietorship: a simple business owned and run by its owner. There are no special legal filings, no extra taxes to be paid, and no dealing with another owner or partner. Of utmost importance to this form of ownership is that the owner is personally liable for everything since there is no legal separation between owner and business. Once the insurance fails, the sole proprietor is still liable to the creditors for debts and for all judgments.

- General partnership: an entity similar to the sole proprietorship, but with just another owner

- Corporation: business treated as a separate legal person that can borrow money, incur debt, and be sued. In a corporation, the owners receive shares of stock for their investments. If the corporation is sued, it is possible that your stock could be seized.

  There are two types of corporations:

  o Regular corporation (also known as a C corporation): a legal entity that is not a pass-through tax entity since it is taxed both at the corporate level on corporate net income and at the share-holder level on distributions such as dividends

  o Small business corporation (also known as an S corporation): a legal entity that eliminates the double taxation of the C corporation. Income and losses are passed directly to the shareholders for tax purposes and are taxed at the individuals' income tax rates. Distributions are not subject to self-employment tax (of 15.3 percent).

  Both types of corporations can trigger a taxable event through the distribution of real property.

B. Establish asset anonymity

- Asset placement

- Privacy trust

C. Prevent lawsuits

- Statutory protection

- Deterrence of workplace lawsuits

D. Preserve financial security

- Insulation of family wealth

- Personal residence trust (PRT)

- Family savings trust (FST)

- Life insurance trust

- Avoidance of unnecessary estate taxes

E. Create artificial poverty

For the purposes of this book, we will segregate real estate investors into groups based on exposure:

A. Active: the investor who has the most exposure

B. Passive: the investor who has the least amount of exposure

5.1   Asset Protection Strategies

Asset protection has two goals: to minimize the risk of potential liability (protect your assets from lawsuits and creditors) and to preserve your assets (continuity and family). The following are asset protection strategies that you might consider implementing with the help of your legal and financial advisers. Some of these suggestions work singularly, but in combination they can provide a higher level of security.

Because real estate is a volatile business, we assume the following: The company is operating as a limited liability company (LLC). If the LLC has only one member for income tax purposes, a grantor trust may be designated as the second member (to protect against a potential charging order or foreclosure). All assets are kept isolated and separate. In other words, each property or project should have its own LLC.

5.2   Active Investor

This investor is completely involved in the day-to-day operations of the business, and the company has employees.

Narrative
The investor has all his or her real estate investments and businesses in LLCs. To minimize liability and lawsuit risks, each of the foregoing is in a separate LLC.

A family limited partnership (FLP) is created to hold and protect assets against lawsuits and business risks. All safe assets (held through a bank, a brokerage, mutual funds, annuity investments, and insurance policies) are transferred into it.

The family home is placed into the personal residence trust (PRT) with the family limited partnership (FLP) as beneficiary.

The family savings trust (FST) is created to hold and protect assets against lawsuits and business risks. All assets (those within the PRT, FLP, and LLCs) are held within this trust. This trust is key in protecting assets and in estate planning.

5.3   Active Investors—Partnership

This investor is completely involved in the day-to-day operations of the business, and the company has employees. Other investments that are owned singularly or together by the husband and wife investors are held in LLCs.

Narrative
The investor has all his or her real estate investments and businesses in a limited partnership (LP).

The family limited partnership (FLP) is created to hold and protect assets against lawsuits and business risks. All safe assets (held through a bank, a brokerage, mutual funds, annuities, and insurance policies) are transferred into it. Assets transferred into an FLP are exchanged for shares in the partnership. Because the FLP owns the assets, those assets are protected from creditors under the Uniform Limited

Partnership Act. However, since you received shares in the FLP, you control the FLP, and so you control the assets within the FLP. There is no market for the shares you receive, so their value is significantly less than the value of the assets exchanged for the shares.

The family home is placed into the personal residence trust (PRT), with the family limited partnership as beneficiary.

The family savings trust (FST) is created to hold and protect assets against lawsuits and business risks. All assets (held in the PRT and FLP) are held within this trust. This trust is key in protecting assets and in estate planning.

5.4   Passive Investor

This investor has nonvolatile investments in limited liability companies and no employees.

Narrative

The investor has all his or her real estate investments and businesses in LLCs. To minimize liability and lawsuit risks, each business is in a separate LLC.

The family limited partnership (FLP) is created to hold and protect assets against lawsuits and business risks. All safe assets (held through a bank, a brokerage, mutual funds, annuity investments, and insurance policies) are transferred into it.

The family home is placed into the personal residence trust (PRT) with the family limited partnership as beneficiary.

The family savings trust (FST) is created to hold and protect assets against lawsuits and business risks. All assets (in the PRT, FLP, and LLCs) are held within this trust. This trust is key in protecting assets and estate planning.

APPENDIX—A
Commonly Used Words and Phrases

Commonly Used Words and Phrases

WORD or PHRASE	MEANING
AB Trust	Instead of leaving property to the surviving spouse, each spouse leaves most of or all of his or her property to an irrevocable trust that can be used for the benefit of the surviving spouse. Because the spouse does not own the property outright, the property is not subject to estate tax when the surviving spouse dies. At most, the surviving spouse may do the following: • Receive all interest or other income from the trust property • Live in the property Spend the money from the trust property in any amount for his or her health, medical (dental, hospital, and nursing), or educational support and maintenance, in accordance with that spouse's accustomed manner of living.
Asset Protection	A preventive measure to protect assets from the uncertainties of an out-of-control legal system in which lawsuits are filed with the intent of obtaining the defendant's assets.
Beneficiary	One or more individuals or organizations specified to be the recipient.
Capital Gain	A result from the sale or exchange of assets used in a trade, or a business, or held for investment. Capital Gains are either short term (assets held for one year or less), or long term (assets held for more than one year and one day).

Charging Order	An order obtained from a court or judge by a judgement creditor, in which the property of the judgement debtor (in any stocks, funds, or real property) stands charged with the payment of the amount for which judgement was obtained with interest and costs. Under most state laws, the only remedy for a creditor pursuing an LLC interest is to obtain a charging order directing that any distribution made to the member/debtor is paid directly to the creditor in lieu of the member. This is usually not a satisfactory solution since the members can vote not to make a distribution. The charging order does not give the creditor any voting rights.
Charitable Estate Planning	An irrevocable trust created by the Trustmaker that transfers assets into a Charitable Remainder Trust, or a Charitable Lead Trust. If the Trustmaker makes the initial transfer while still alive, the Trustmaker will receive a charitable income tax deduction in the year the transfer is made. If the transfer occurs after the Trustmaker's death, then the Trustmaker's estate will receive a charitable estate deduction.
Corporations	A corporation is a company or group of people authorized to act as a single entity (legally a person) and recognized as such in law. A corporation is a taxpaying entity and must file an annual tax return, and pay taxes on its income. If those earning are distributed to the shareholders it is treated as a dividend. A major problem with the corporation format for small business is that the shareholders, officers and directors will be named in any lawsuit against the corporation.

Crummey Power	When a donor contributes to an irrevocable trust, the beneficiaries must be notified that the funds can be withdrawn within a certain time (no less than 30 days). When the beneficiary does not withdraw the funds, they go back to the trust and are then subject to the annual gift tax exclusion. The donor will usually inform the beneficiary of his or her intentions to use the Crummey power, so that the beneficiary declines to withdraw the gift when given the opportunity.
Equity Reduction Plan	A specialized form of asset protection designed to protect equity in real estate or business assets from potential future claim. The ERP can be used as its own entity or in conjunction with other asset protection vehicles.
Estate Tax	An estate tax is a tax imposed on the decedent's estate. The executor fills out a single estate tax return and pays the tax out of the estate's funds. The heirs will only be held liable for the tax if the executor fails to pay it.

The estate tax can be especially harsh for very high net worth individuals who fail to plan to minimize its effect. |
| Family Trust | A trust established by a family member for the benefit of members of the family group. It provides a legal mechanism to pass family assets to future generations, and can provide a means of accessing favorable taxation treatment. The trust can assist in protecting the group's assets from the liabilities of one or more of the family members. |
| Federal Estate Tax | The federal estate tax affects those with very large estates. The amount that an individual can leave ($XX million) without paying estate |

	tax (in addition to assets left to a spouse, which are not subject to estate tax). Couples can combine their assets, without owing federal estate tax. See IRS regulations for current exemptions.

Federal Estate Tax Exemption Levels

YEAR	TAX RATE	EXEMPTION LEVEL
2013	40%	5.25 million
2014	40%	5.34 million
2015	40%	5.43 million
2016	40%	5.45 million

Fraudulent Conveyance	The act of intentionally conveying assets with the intent of delaying, hindering or defrauding creditors, or constructive fraudulent conveyance.
Grantor	An individual who conveys or transfers ownership of property.
Inheritance Tax	An inheritance tax is a tax imposed on the people (beneficiaries) who receive property from the deceased. The tax is calculated separately for each beneficiary, and each beneficiary is responsible for paying his or her own inheritance taxes. Those states that have inheritance taxes frequently tax spouses and children of the deceased at lower rates than other heirs.
Irrevocable Life Insurance Trust	A method of removing the value of property from an estate so that the property cannot be taxed upon the person's death. The beneficiaries of the trust receive this asset tax free.
Irrevocable Trust	A type of trust that cannot be changed after the agreement has been signed, or a revocable trust that becomes irrevocable after the Trust maker dies. An irrevocable trust has asset protection benefits.

Living Trust	A trust that exists and is operational during your lifetime. A living Trust maybe revocable or non-revocable. A trust takes precedence over a will.
Revocable Living Trust	Also, called a **Revocable Trust** or **Living Trust**, is a type of trust that can be changed at any time. Changes are made through a *trust amendment*, or can be revoked and completely changed through an *amendment and restatement*. A revocable trust has no asset protection. Advantages of a revocable living trust are: • It automatically avoids all probate of the property; • Avoids all legal fees and expenses associated with probate; • Provides for property management or disbursement; • Assures uninterrupted income and access to principal for beneficiaries; • Maintains privacy; • Eliminates delays in settling the estate • For US citizens, it protects up to $1,500,000 and $3,000,000 for a married couple.
Settlor	The trustor, grantor, donor or creator.
Trust	A relationship whereby property (real, tangible and intangible) is managed by one person (persons or organization) for the benefit of another. A trust is created by a settlor. This entity is essential in creating various strategies for accomplishing asset protection, estate

	planning, and privacy. The trust avoids probate and can be used to reduce income and estate taxes. A trust takes precedence over a will.
Trust Agreement	The document that specifies what the trustee is required to do, how to hold it, and who is to receive any benefits paid by the trust.
Trustor	The person who puts money or other property in a trust.
Trustee	The person or organization who agrees to hold the property according to terms
Trust Company	A company in the business of managing assets. The company makes investment decisions for the trust, and distributes funds according to the terms of the trust agreement. This service can be useful for an elderly or minor beneficiary.
Corporations	A corporation is a company or group of people authorized to act as a single entity (legally a person) and recognized as such in law. A corporation is a taxpaying entity and must file an annual tax return, and pay taxes on its income. If those earning are distributed to the shareholders it is treated as a dividend. A major problem with the corporation format for small business is that the shareholders, officers and directors will be named in any lawsuit against the corporation.
Crummey Power	When a donor contributes to an irrevocable trust, the beneficiaries must be notified that the funds can be withdrawn within a certain time (no less than 30 days). When the beneficiary does not withdraw the funds, they go back to the trust and are then subject to the annual gift tax exclusion. The donor will usually inform the beneficiary of his or her intentions to use the Crummey power, so that the beneficiary

	declines to withdraw the gift when given the opportunity.
Equity Reduction Plan	A specialized form of asset protection designed to protect equity in real estate or business assets from potential future claim. The ERP can be used as its own entity or in conjunction with other asset protection vehicles.
Estate Tax	An estate tax is a tax imposed on the decedent's estate. The executor fills out a single estate tax return and pays the tax out of the estate's funds. The heirs will only be held liable for the tax if the executor fails to pay it. The estate tax can be especially harsh for very high net worth individuals who fail to plan to minimize its effect.
Family Trust	A trust established by a family member for the benefit of members of the family group. It provides a legal mechanism to pass family assets to future generations, and can provide a means of accessing favorable taxation treatment. The trust can assist in protecting the group's assets from the liabilities of one or more of the family members.
Federal Estate Tax	The federal estate tax affects those with very large estates. The amount that an individual can leave ($XX million) without paying estate tax (in addition to assets left to a spouse, which are not subject to estate tax). Couples can combine their assets, without owing federal estate tax. See IRS regulations for current exemptions.

Federal Estate Tax	YEAR	TAX RATE	EXEMPTION LEVEL
	2013	40%	5.25 million
	2014	40%	5.34 million

Exemption Levels	2015	40%	5.43 million
	2016	40%	5.45 million
Fraudulent Conveyance	The act of intentionally conveying assets with the intent of delaying, hindering or defrauding creditors, or constructive fraudulent conveyance.		
Grantor	An individual who conveys or transfers ownership of property.		
Inheritance Tax	An inheritance tax is a tax imposed on the people (beneficiaries) who receive property from the deceased. The tax is calculated separately for each beneficiary, and each beneficiary is responsible for paying his or her own inheritance taxes. Those states that have inheritance taxes frequently tax spouses and children of the deceased at lower rates than other heirs.		
Irrevocable Life Insurance Trust	A method of removing the value of property from an estate so that the property cannot be taxed upon the person's death. The beneficiaries of the trust receive this asset tax free.		
Irrevocable Trust	A type of trust that cannot be changed after the agreement has been signed, or a revocable trust that becomes irrevocable after the Trust maker dies. An irrevocable trust has asset protection benefits.		
Living Trust	A trust that exists and is operational during your lifetime. A living Trust maybe revocable or non-revocable. A trust takes precedence over a will.		
Revocable Living Trust	Also, called a **Revocable Trust** or **Living Trust**, is a type of trust that can be changed at any time. Changes are made through a *trust amendment,* or can be revoked and completely changed through an *amendment and*		

	restatement. A revocable trust has no asset protection. Advantages of a revocable living trust are: • It automatically avoids all probate of the property; • Avoids all legal fees and expenses associated with probate; • Provides for property management or disbursement; • Assures uninterrupted income and access to principal for beneficiaries; • Maintains privacy; • Eliminates delays in settling the estate • For US citizens, it protects up to $1,500,000 and $3,000,000 for a married couple.
Settlor	The trustor, grantor, donor or creator.
Trust	A relationship whereby property (real, tangible and intangible) is managed by one person (persons or organization) for the benefit of another. A trust is created by a settlor. This entity is essential in creating various strategies for accomplishing asset protection, estate planning, and privacy. The trust avoids probate and can be used to reduce income and estate taxes. A trust takes precedence over a will.
Trust Agreement	The document that specifies what the trustee is required to do, how to hold it, and who is to receive any benefits paid by the trust.
Trustor	The person who puts money or other property in a trust.

Trustee	The person or organization who agrees to hold the property according to terms
Trust Company	A company in the business of managing assets. The company makes investment decisions for the trust, and distributes funds according to the terms of the trust agreement. This service can be useful for an elderly or minor beneficiary.

APPENDIX—B
Asset Protection Illustrations

Figure B-1

The Basic Plan

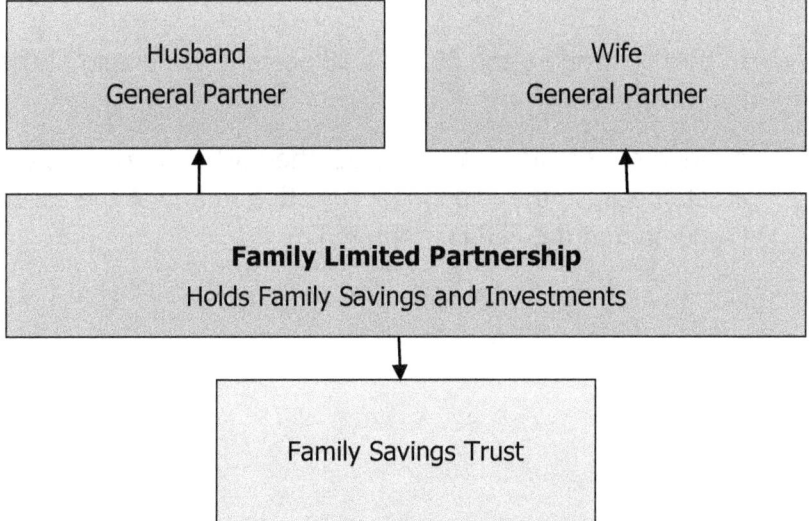

The Basic Plan

A. Create a family limited partnership (FLP) in which the husband and wife are general partners, each owning 1 percent in the FLP.

- After setting up the FLP, "safe assets" are transferred into it.

- When the assets are transferred into the FLP, the husband and wife no longer own those assets directly; instead, they own a controlling interest in the FLP, which owns the assets.

- As general partners, they have complete management and control over the affairs of the partnership and can buy or sell assets as wanted.

B. Create the family savings trust (FST). This trust is intended to hold and protect assets against lawsuits and business risks. A family savings trust is extremely flexible, and almost any asset protection and estate planning goal can be accomplished through it.

- In this illustration, the FST has 98 percent ownership of the FLP contents.

- A judgment creditor cannot touch the husband's or wife's assets because they no longer hold title to any of the assets. Ownership of the FLP is in the FST.

Figure B-2

The Basic Plan with a Personal Residence Trust

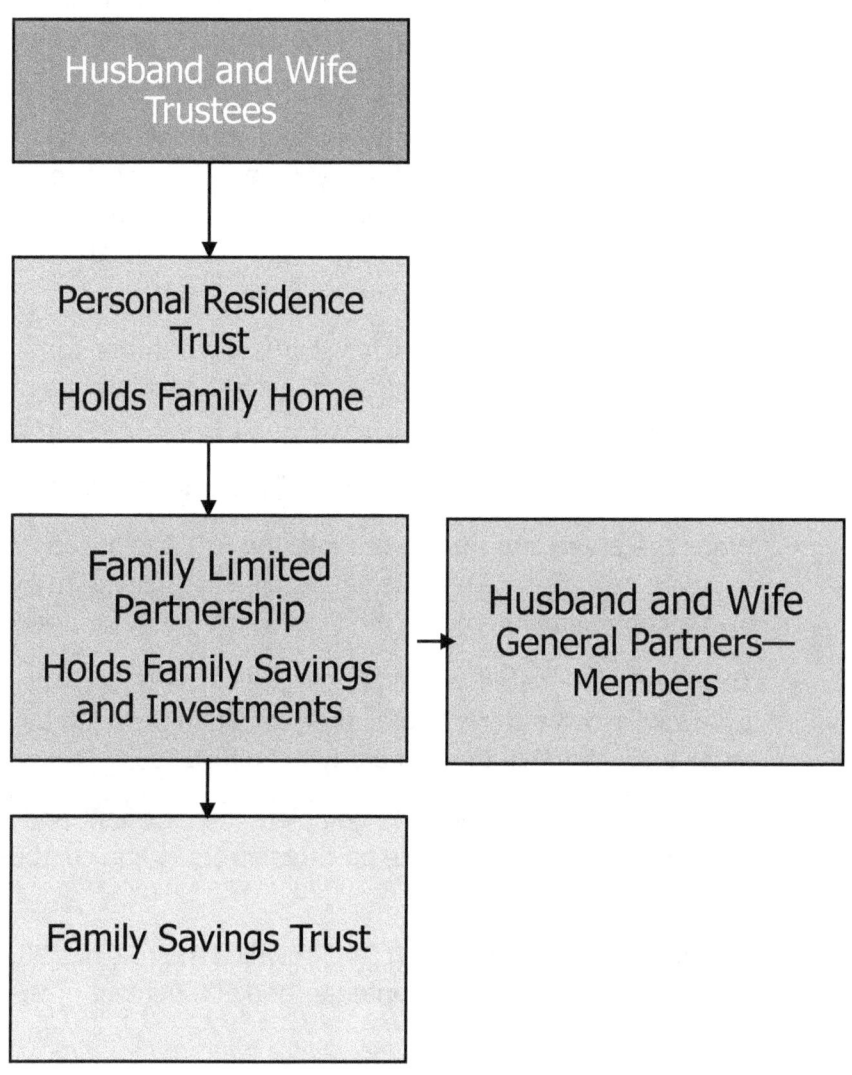

The Basic Plan with the Personal Residence Trust

A. Create the personal residence trust (PRT), in which you place your personal home. The reason for this is that your personal residence is entitled to certain tax advantages that will not be available if the home is placed in the FLP. These advantages are the mortgage interest deduction and the $250,000-per-spouse capital gain exclusion.

- In this grantor-type trust, both you and your spouse are trustees of the trust. As trustees, you have full power to buy, sell, or refinance the property. The interest deduction is reported directly on your tax return, and all the other advantages of home ownership are preserved.

B. Create the family limited partnership (FLP), in which the husband and wife are general partners, each owning 1 percent in the FLP.

- After setting up the FLP, "safe assets" are transferred into it.

- When the assets are transferred into the FLP, the husband and wife no longer own those assets directly. Instead, they own a controlling interest in the FLP, which owns the assets.

- The FLP is designated as the beneficiary of the (PRT). This allows your home to receive all the protection provided by these entities without creating any tax difficulties.

- As general partners, you have complete management and control over the affairs of the partnership (FLP) and can buy or sell assets as wanted.

C. Create the family savings trust (FST), in which the FST has 98 percent ownership of the FLP contents (and 100 percent of the LLC).

- A judgment creditor cannot touch the husband's or wife's assets because they no longer hold title to any of the assets. Ownership of the FLP (and LLC) is in the FSP.

D. Create a position in case of foreclosure on the FLP interest: The law generally provides that a judgment creditor of a partner can obtain a charging order against the debtor's partnership interest. The charging order gives the debtor a right to any distributions from the partnership to the debtor partner and remains in effect until the creditor has been paid in full or until the time limit for collecting the judgment has expired.

- A popular alternative for asset protection and for owning an FLP interest is to transfer the ownership into a trust that is designed for this purpose, such as an FST.

- The key to solving this problem is to form one or more FLPs or other entities (such as offshore limited liability companies).

Figure B-3

The Basic Plan with a Limited Liability Company

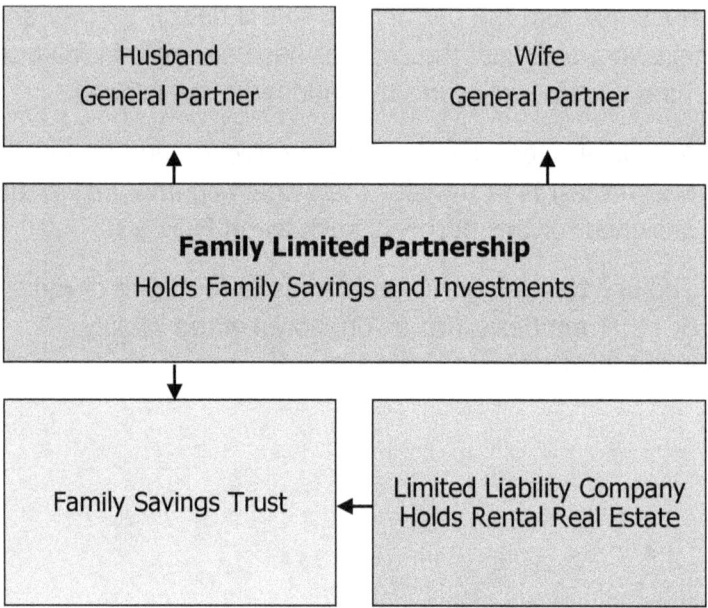

The Basic Plan with a Limited Liability Company

A. Create the family limited partnership (FLP) in which the husband and wife are general partners, each owning 1 percent in the FLP.

- After setting up the FLP, "safe assets" are transferred into it.

- When the assets are transferred into the FLP, the husband and wife no longer own these assets directly. Instead, they own a controlling interest in the FLP, which owns the assets.

- As general partners, they have complete management and control over the affairs of the partnership and can buy or sell assets as wanted.

B. Create the family savings trust (FST), in which the FST has 98 percent ownership of the FLP contents (and 100 percent of the LLC).

- A judgment creditor cannot touch the husband's or wife's assets because they no longer hold title to any of the assets. Ownership of the FLP (and LLC) is in the FSP.

C. Transfer 100 percent ownership from the LLC into the FSP.

- The LLC is treated like a partnership for tax purposes. All the income and deductions flow through to the members' personal tax returns.

- The LLC gives the members more protection than a corporation since a corporation will not offer protection of the property from outside claims and from lawsuits against the members who are unrelated to the property. In a corporation, the creditor can simply seize the stock that is owned and reach the commercial property by dissolving the company. (Therefore, it is not advisable to hold investment real estate in a corporation.)

D. Foreclosure of FLP or LLC interest: The law generally provides that a judgment creditor of a partner can obtain a charging order against the debtor's partnership interest. The charging order gives the debtor a right to any distributions from the partnership to the debtor partner and remains in effect until the creditor has been paid in full or until the time limit for collecting the judgment has expired.

- A popular alternative for asset protection and for owning an FLP interest is to transfer the ownership into a trust that is designed for this purpose, such as an FST.

- The key to solving this problem is to form one or more FLPs, LLCs, or other entities (such as offshore limited liability companies).

APPENDIX—C
Asset Protection Vehicles Used

NOTE: State and federal laws change frequently, and the following information may not reflect recent changes in the laws. For current tax and legal advice, please consult with an accountant and an attorney.

BUSINESS

The Limited Liability Company

General: The limited liability company (LLC) is a legal entity created by state statute. The LLC combines the best features of corporations and partnerships while eliminating many of the complexities and problems of each. The LLC provides members with protection from liability and debts incurred by the LLC, and property held cannot be seized by the creditor of a member.

For creditors of a single-member LLC, there must be more than one legal owner membership interest in the LLC to protect it against charging orders or foreclosure. This can be accomplished by designating a grantor trust as the second member.

All the profits and losses of the LLC are allocated among the members as agreed to in the operating agreement. The LLC pays no income tax since the income and deductions flow directly to the members' personal tax returns.

The LLC is viewed as the best way to insulate risky assets such as an office building, rental property, and other business ventures you might undertake.

Note: Single-member LLCs do not offer the same protection as a multiple (two or more members) LLC since the creditor may be able to take control of the single-member LLC because there are no other members whose interests need to be protected regarding the charging order. Use a grantor trust as explained above.

The Limited Partnership

General: The limited partnership (LP) is a legal entity created by state statute. The LP consists of two or more persons, and there is at least one general partner and one limited partner. The general partner has unlimited personal liability (unless the company is set up as a limited liability company), and the limited partner's liability is limited to the amount of investment.

The general partner or partners have management control, share the right to use partnership property, share the profits of the firm in predefined proportions, and have joint and several liabilities for the debts of the partnership. The limited partners have no management authority (unless they obligate themselves under a separate contract such as a guaranty) and are not liable for the debts of the partnership. The LP interest is considered a security by law. It can be transferred to a third party, but general partners and other limited partners have the right of first refusal.

Partnership interests are given a significant level of protection through the charging order. The charging order limits the creditor of a debtor-partner or a debtor-member to the debtor's share of distributions without conferring on the creditor any voting or management rights.

If the LP meets minimum criteria related to limited liability, centralized management, duration, and transferability of ownership, it can enjoy the benefits of pass-through taxation. Otherwise, it will be taxed as a corporation.

The main problem with a limited partnership is the unlimited liability of the general partners for the debts of the partnership. The LLC solves this problem!

The LP is most often used as a vehicle for raising capital for real estate investment projects, and it is used by businesses that focus on a single or limited-term project.

Equity Reduction Plan

An equity reduction plan (ERP) is a highly effective form of asset protection. Depending on the circumstances and the types of assets involved, an ERP can be used by itself or in combination with other asset-protection techniques. ERPs are designed to protect equity in real estate or business assets from a potential future claim. When movement of an asset is impossible or impractical, an ERP can move the equity or value into a protected position. Ownership of the underlying property remains the same, and it need not be transferred.

- An ERP protects the equity in a property from a claim arising out of the property itself.

- An ERP avoids a transfer of real estate ownership and potential problems with increased property taxes, transfer taxes, and due-on-sale clauses from a lender.

- Owners of multiple properties can avoid the inconvenience and cost associated with forming several LLCs.

- Accounts receivable usually cannot be transferred out of a professional practice because of accounting problems and insurance company restrictions. An ERP is the only way to protect the cash-flow cycle of billing and collection.

- The inventory, equipment, and intellectual property in a business are essential for operations and future success of the business. An ERP is designed to avoid disruption or loss of the business by protecting these assets.

- Valuable but unproductive equity in real estate, accounts receivable, and business property can be leveraged for business or investment purposes. These dormant assets can be put to work in an ERP, enhancing asset protection and generating additional income.

Trademarks, Patents, and Copyrights

Trademarks, patents, and copyrights are valuable assets that should not be owned directly by the operating entity. A separate company can own these assets and make them available through a licensing agreement. Here, the objective is to protect these assets in the event of a judgment against the corporation.

Employee Handbook

Your employee handbook can help to provide you with asset protection against workplace lawsuits by including in it your company's policies on confidentiality, nondisclosure, and alternative dispute resolution. Through the inclusion of the foregoing, it will help to deter against unauthorized disclosure of your private and proprietary information and allow disputes to be settled through arbitration in lieu of costly court proceedings.

The handbook works well as part of your overall asset protection plan. Should arbitration fail to resolve a workplace dispute, your asset protection plan will protect your assets and minimize the economic incentive to sue.

You can review information about arbitration on the American Arbitration Association website at http://www.adr.org.

Insurance

Have your company purchase "key man insurance." This insurance will help to compensate the business for financial losses that arise from the death or extended incapacity of a member of the business.

PERSONAL

The Family Limited Partnership

General: The family limited partnership (FLP) is a device used for providing a high degree of protection for family wealth from lawsuits. When properly designed, it will offer significant income and estate tax savings and advantages.

This type of limited partnership consists of one or more general partners (husband and wife) and one or more limited partners (children and grandchildren). The same person can be both a general and limited partner if there are two legal persons in the partnership.

The general partner is responsible for the management of the affairs of the partnership and has unlimited personal liability for all debts and obligations. Limited partners have no personal liability and will lose only the amount contributed to the partnership.

Tax treatment: A partnership is not a tax-paying entity. The partnership files an annual information tax return but does not pay tax on its net income. Each partner's share of income is passed from the partnership to the partner, and that partner declares his or her share of income on his or her own tax return.

Lawsuit protection: Typically, the FLP is set up so that the husband and wife are each general partners (members), and each owns a 1 percent interest of the partnership. The remaining interests (98 percent) are in the form of limited partnership interests held in a family savings trust. Under the Uniform Limited Partnership Act, the creditor of a partner cannot reach into the partnership and take specific partnership assets. The creditor has no rights to any property that is held by the partnership.

As general partners, the husband and wife have management and control over the affairs of the partnership and can buy or sell assets, can retain funds from the sale of any assets, and can distribute proceeds to the partners.

Bank and brokerage accounts (safe assets) are held in the FLP.

Mutual funds, annuity investments, and insurance policies are held in the FLP.

Dangerous assets (those that may produce liability), such as real estate and other business interests, are held in the family savings trust, which is owned by the FLP. The partners own a "controlling" interest in the FLP, which owns the assets.

Estate tax benefit: The FLP can be used to shift the value of assets out of your estate through a program of gifting limited partnership interests to your children or other family members.

Note: The family limited partnership is not a stand-alone device for an asset protection plan.

The Living Trust
General: The entity known as a trust is the foundation of estate planning. It is essential in creating various strategies for accomplishing asset protection, estate planning, and privacy benefits.

The trust is a written agreement between a settlor and a trustee. This agreement provides that the settlor will transfer certain assets to the trustee, and the trustee will hold those assets for the benefit of the named beneficiaries. A trust may have one or more trustees who are responsible for administering and carrying out the terms of the trust. The beneficiaries are those who are entitled to trust income or principal either currently or at some time in the future.

The Revocable Living Trust
This is a trust established during the lifetime of the settlor that can be revoked or canceled at any time. (Testamentary trusts, those created upon the settlor's death, do not avoid probate.)

    A. Avoiding probate: A revocable trust (or irrevocable trust) that is properly drafted and funded will avoid probate. Any property that has not been transferred into the trust will be subject to probate. The trust document, like a will, provides for the disposition of trust assets upon the death of the settlor.

B. Funding: The trust must be properly funded. Transfer legal title of all family assets into the trust prior to a spouse's death.

- For real estate, the change in title is accomplished by executing and recording a deed to the property.

- Bank and brokerage accounts can be transferred by changing the name on the accounts to reflect the trust as the new owner.

- Shares of stocks and bonds can be transferred by notifying the transfer agent for the issuing company and requesting that the certificates be reissued in the name of the trust.

- Other types of property can be transferred by a simple written declaration called an assignment.

The living trust can be funded indirectly by transferring interest in other entities—i.e., if you hold your property in a family limited partnership (FLP) or limited liability company (LLC), the living trust can hold your shares in those companies.

Example: A husband and wife create a revocable trust with both as initial trustees and beneficiaries of the trust. The trust provides that during their joint lifetimes the trust may be revoked at any time. Upon the death of either spouse, the trust becomes irrevocable, and the surviving spouse becomes the sole trustee. When the surviving spouse dies, the trust property passes according to the wishes expressed in the trust document.

C. Estate taxes: The trust must contain the appropriate provisions to minimize federal taxes payable upon the death of either spouse. The unified tax credit allows each spouse to transfer up to the exemption amount to children or anyone else free of any federal estate taxes.

A properly drawn revocable trust takes advantage of this benefit by creating two trusts—known as the A trust and the B trust. In a large estate, the B trust will be funded with the exemption amount, and the balance will go into the A trust. From the A trust, the surviving spouse will have the right to all income for life plus a power to use any portion of the principal that he or she desires. The B trust will generally provide that the surviving spouse is entitled to all income during his or her life plus the right to use principal for health, education, maintenance, and support.

D. Income tax treatment: For tax purposes, a revocable trust is a grantor trust and does not provide any income tax savings. No annual tax return is required to be filed. All income and loss incurred by the trust is reported on the husband and wife's tax returns.

E. Revocable trust and asset protection: This trust does not provide any protection of assets from judgment creditors. It is ignored for creditor purposes like it is for tax purposes. In most states, the law provides that if a settlor has the right to revoke the trust, all the assets are treated as if they are owned by the settlor.

F. Gifts between spouses: These gifts qualify for the unlimited marital deduction, which eliminates federal gift taxes on these kinds of transfers.

G. Community property: In community property states, each spouse's interest is subject to the claims of the other spouse's creditors unless the separate property of a spouse will not be subject to the claims of the creditors of the other spouse.

H. Equal division of property: Marital property can be divided according to a written agreement that states that each spouse is to hold one-half of all marital property as that spouse's own separate property. Once divided, two separate revocable trusts can be established, one for each spouse.

I. Gifts to family members: This is a useful tool that may accomplish a variety of asset and estate planning objectives. Properly structured, giving to one's children or grandchildren can result in minimization of estate and income taxes besides achieving a significant degree of lawsuit protection.

Advantages of gift giving are as follows:

- Lifetime gifts reduce the size of one's estate and consequently minimize the ultimate amount of estate tax.

- You will save substantially on estate tax rates.

- A gift-giving program may also produce some annual income tax savings.

- The program will provide lawsuit protection.

- If the gift is not fraudulent, it cannot be touched by a judgment creditor of the husband or wife.

The Personal Residence Trust

General: This is a grantor trust permitted under the Internal Revenue Code. The personal residence trust (PRT) gives the trustees (husband and wife) the right to buy and use the house. The home cannot be sold during the term of occupancy by the trustees. The mortgage interest is reported on the trustees' income tax return, and all advantages of home ownership are retained, including the capital gains exclusion.

To protect the asset, legal rights must be limited in some manner, or a judge can order the property turned over to a plaintiff with a judgment against you. In limiting your rights, your interest may have no value to a prospective creditor. Some popular solutions to create this scenario are as follows:

- The trust reserves your right to live in the residence for a period of time (twenty or thirty years) and then turns ownership over to your children. This method can also provide estate tax benefits.

- Alternately, the PRT owns the home, and you lease the home for a specific number of years. The rent that you pay goes to the trust.

This estate planning strategy is known as a "qualified personal residence trust" and is specifically sanctioned under section 2702 (b) of the Internal Revenue Code.

    A. Advantages: The PRT gives tax advantages that would not be available in the FLP or LLC. The LP/LLC is designated as the beneficiary of the trust, thereby receiving all the protection from that entity.

The Family Savings Trust

General: This is a flexible trust that can be designed to hold and protect assets against lawsuits and business risks while achieving tax savings and family estate planning goals. The family savings trust (FST) can hold your home, accounts receivable, savings and brokerage accounts, and life insurance trust. Or the trust can own entities such as limited liability companies, a family limited partnership, and a personal residence trust.

The family savings trust should contain specific language to protect the following:

- Your home while preserving the tax benefits associated with it

- Your LLC/FLP interest from a charging order or foreclosure

- Your accounts receivable or other business assets with an equity reduction strategy

- Savings and brokerage accounts

- The degree of privacy that you wish to have

- The provision of estate planning features of a living trust as well as advanced estate tax savings

A. Income tax planning: One of the key considerations in creating the FSP is determining who is responsible for taxable income. Are the parents responsible for putting the taxable income on their returns, or are the children responsible since they fall into a low tax bracket, or is the tax on the income paid by a different entity such as a corporation or an LLC?

Is the trust designed as a grantor or nongrantor trust per sections 671–679 of the Internal Revenue Code? The difference is that when the trust is treated as a grantor trust, all the income is required to be included on the tax return of the person or persons who establish the trust.

Example: The assets of the FST consist of a 98 percent limited partnership interest in an FLP, and the FLP holds investments the husband and wife created. Who reports and pays tax on that amount depends on whether the FST is considered a grantor trust or a nongrantor trust. If it is a grantor trust, then the FST is ignored for federal tax purposes, and all its income is reported on the parents' tax return. If the FST is a nongrantor trust, then the income is included on the tax return of the FST or, if distributed, on the return of the beneficiaries.

B. Protection of your residence: Features that protect the family home are a key component in the FSP. We must protect the equity in the home above the homestead amount while preserving the tax benefits and the continued right to use and enjoy the house. The trust use is a "grantor trust," and if certain language is used in the trust document, the IRS will treat you, not the trust, as the owner of the property.

C. Asset protection for a limited term of years: A popular strategy is the establishment of a trust that is designed to last for a specified term of years, with the trust assets returned to the settlor or the trust beneficiary at the end of the term.

The primary goals here are the following:

- Protect your savings from any lawsuit or claim

- Make sure the funds are available when you retire

- Let the FLP pay for the children's education

Life Insurance Trust

General: Death benefits from life insurance policies are not subject to income tax, but the benefits could be counted as part of your taxable estate. If your estate is valued at more than the exemption level (see the table in Appendix-A) in place at the time of death, the government will provide your beneficiaries a *big* tax bill.

A. The solution: An irrevocable life insurance trust is a tool that can help beneficiaries erase the tax burden. The trust "owns" the policy, pays the premiums, and gives the death benefit to your beneficiaries when you die. By placing ownership of the policy with a trust rather than with the insured, the death benefit is removed from the estate. If this drops your estate value below the exemption level *(see chart)*, you've freed your beneficiaries from a big tax bill.

When a policy is held by the FSP with the appropriate language governing the ownership of the policy and the administration and disposition of the proceeds, the trust keeps the policy out of your estate, free of estate tax, thereby freeing the entire amount of the proceeds for your family. Also, when a policy is held by the trust, the cash value and the proceeds are protected from potential lawsuits and claims.

Premium payments can be made by making cash payments, or "gifts," to the trust. You can avoid paying gift taxes on amounts up to $14,000 per year since your policy is in a trust. This tax loophole is called "Crummey Power."

B. Drawbacks: With the life insurance trust, there are certain drawbacks:

- You cannot borrow from the policy.
- The trust is irrevocable.
- You cannot change the beneficiaries of the policy.

The Privacy Trust

This is a descriptive name for legal strategies designed to achieve financial privacy. A privacy trust can be created for the sole legitimate purpose of concealing the ownership of assets (business and personal) from public view to avoid privacy intrusions. Since the trust is revocable, the law provides that the trust can be reached in a collection proceeding. Although most lawsuits will be discouraged by the secrecy attributes, if you own *dangerous assets* or have substantial liability risks, you should consider a strategy that combines asset protection features, such as an LLC or FLP, with the privacy trust. The interest in those entities would be owned by the trust.

Privacy trusts are identified by the name of the trust, the name of the trustee, and a tax identification number issued by the Internal Revenue Service. Your name and social security number are not used to identify the trust—e.g., ABC Trust #5555.

In addition to the privacy benefits, all the typical estate planning advantages can be achieved. The trust performs the same role as a living trust to avoid probate, minimize estate taxes, and pass your property per your requests.

APPENDIX—D
Legacy

Grantor Retained Annuity Trust

General: A grantor retained annuity trust (GRAT) is a method for the grantor to transfer commercial property (an asset) into an irrevocable trust while maintaining control over the asset and receiving distributions from the asset for a fixed term of years. Currently, the annuity payment may be increased up to 20 percent per annum.

Upon expiration of the annuity term, ownership of the GRAT passes to the remainder beneficiaries at no additional gift tax cost. If the grantor dies before the trust period ends, the assets in the GRAT are included in the grantor's estate, eliminating any potential gift tax benefit. (This is the GRAT's main weakness.)

A GRAT is a tax-efficient way for a grantor with an appreciating estate and potential significant tax exposure to maximize his or her family wealth transfer. It works best in a low-interest-rate environment as a lower interest rate increases the value of the annuity retained by the grantor and therefore reduces the value of the gift of the remainder interest.

Charitable Remainder Trust (CRT)

A Charitable Remainder Trust is a special tax-exempt irrevocable trust arrangement written to comply with federal tax laws and regulations. You transfer cash or assets (especially appreciated assets) to the trust and may receive income for life or, if you choose, a certain term of years (not to exceed 20). In fact, the income can be paid over your life, your spouse's life and even your children's and grandchildren's lives.

General: This trust is an irrevocable trust with the beneficiary being a nonprofit charity(s) of your choice. You benefit from a reliable lifetime income stream[1], and you also receive a charitable deduction at the time

---

[1] Income choices are:
- Fixed percentage of the trust's assets (Charitable Remainder Unitrust).
- Fixed income (Charitable Remainder Annuity Trust).
- Postponed income (with tax deduction NOW).

the trust is established. Because a charitable remainder trust is exempt from capital gains, no tax is due when the asset is sold or when the remainder is donated to the charity. In the end, *a minimum of 10 percent of the original value must be left in the trust* to benefit the selected charity (applies to Charitable Remainder Unitrust only).

Since many people are not comfortable donating a major asset to charity at the expense of their heirs, there is a remedy for this. The charitable remainder trust can purchase a life insurance policy on the annuitant that is payable to the heirs. Effectively, the life insurance payoff becomes their inheritance.

- With the Life Insurance Trust the proceeds will not be included in your estate, so you avoid estate tax. You can keep the proceeds in the trust for years, making periodic distributions to your children and grandchildren[2]. Any proceeds kept in the trust are protected from irresponsible spending and creditors.

- Insurance proceeds are available immediately to your heirs. The proceeds avoid estate taxes and are free from probate and income taxes.

Charities: The types of charities that the IRS recognizes deductions for are:

A. A community chest, corporation, trust, fund, or foundation organized or created in or under the laws of the United States, including Puerto Rico.

- Religious
- Charitable

---

[2] NO. An income beneficiary may not be added. However, when the trust is drafted, it may allow for a contingent beneficiary through a special provision. The contingent beneficiary may be removed only by the donor's will and may not be replaced.

- Education

- Scientific

- Literary

- The prevention of cruelty to children or animals

- Certain organizations that foster national or international amateur sports competition

B. War veterans' organizations

C. Domestic fraternal societies, orders, and associations operating under the lodge system

D. Certain nonprofit cemetery companies or corporations

E. An Indian tribal government or any of its subdivisions that perform substantial government functions

Advantages of charitable remainder trusts are as follows:

- Eliminates capital gains taxes on appreciated property

- Creates a stream of income without the risk of triggering taxes or default on installment sales

- Provides a charitable tax deduction in the year it is established and funded[3]

- Removes highly appreciated property from the estate

- Serves to fund a life insurance policy to provide heirs with a replacement inheritance

---

[3] The deduction is based upon the estimated present value of the remainder interest that will ultimately go to the charity.

Note: Charitable remainder trusts (CRTs) should be designed by an attorney due to the long-term implications and irrevocability of the trust.

The two most popular types of charitable remainder trusts are as follows:

- Charitable remainder annuity trusts (CRATs): These entities pay a fixed income each year corresponding to a percentage of the original investment (5 percent minimum to 50 percent maximum[4]). Income is paid each year regardless of how much the CRAT earns from its investments. If investment returns are insufficient to provide the required income, principal will be used to pay the required amount.

- Charitable remainder unit trusts (CRUTs): CRUTs do not require that the principal be used to sustain the income stream. However, the option is available. The CRUT provides more flexibility in how income streams are paid. The CRUT may increase with inflation or may not pay the appropriate amount in some years. Variations on how the CRUT can make payments include the following:

  o Payments can be made as a set percentage of the annual value of the trust (may include paying out principal).

  o Payments can be made out of income only, so the CRUT does not pay anything if it does not obtain an income from investments. Principal is not used to make annual income payments. Provisions can be made to have missed income made up in future years.

Charitable remainder trusts have these tax implications: Capital gains tax is deferred until the beneficiary receives payments from the CRT, and the taxes are slowly paid with inflated dollars. Because the CRT

---

[4] These payout percentages are required by the IRS.

continues to invest and generate earnings, the tax components in the CRT payments can be complex. The CRT can be expected to earn a combination of tax-exempt income and taxable income. The CRT does not pay taxes itself; you, the beneficiary, pay them. The components of the payments you can expect are as follows:

- Ordinary income

- Tax-exempt income

- Income for which capital gains tax is paid

- Income that is a return of principal

Note: the proportion in each year's payments will vary because of changing returns of investment in each category from year to year.

Tax Favorable Charities and Nonprofit Organizations

A. Wealth Replacement Trust
General: For those that still want their heirs to have capital a life insurance policy payable to the heirs is a good choice.

- The life insurance policy does not need to be as high in value as the donated property, since the highly-appreciated assets would have paid a substantial tax that could not be passed to the heirs.

- Any estate tax would further reduce the property's value that did pass to the heirs.

Benefits: It may be possible to establish another trust that receives the proceeds from the insurance policy so that proceeds pass to the heirs outside the estate.

B. Charitable Lead Trust (CLT)
General: The charity receives the income interest, the assets remain in the CLT for a set term, and at the end of the term, the assets pass to the donor's heirs either free of gift or estate tax or at a substantially reduced rate.

Benefits: It reduces the size of the taxable estate, and it retains property in the family, often with reduced gift taxes.

C. Retained Life Estate
General: this charity gifting method allows you to obtain the charitable tax deduction during your lifetime and spend the rest of your years in the home. Ownership of the home is transferred to the charity in exchange for the tax deduction.

D. Charitable Gift Annuity
The charitable gift annuity provides the donor with an income stream and tax deduction in exchange for a donation. In lieu of a trust, this is a contract between the annuitant and the charity. The income stream is backed by the total assets of the charity, and not by the value of the contribution.

Generally, the American Council on Gift Annuities establishes the rate of return. Rates of return increase as the age of the annuitant increases. The payments are partially tax free to the annuitant since they are not income.

E. Pooled Income Fund
General: This fund provides a lifetime income stream with tax favorable treatment. Contributions to pooled income funds are treated favorably for income tax, gift tax, and estate tax.

Under this fund, your charitable donation is commingled with other donors in exchange for approportionate annual payment based on the fund's investment earnings. At the end of the donor's life, the remaining value of their portion is removed from the fund and given to the charity.

Benefits: Tax benefits include

- No IRS recognition of capital gain on donated property

- Property with debt owed realizes a capital gain to the donor in the form of debt forgiven

- Deductible for income, gift, and estate purposes based on value at the time of donation

For estate taxes the donor's value of the fund is first included in the estate, and then excluded based on the donation to charity, effectively removing it from the estate

CHARITABLE OPTIONS COMPARISON			
Charitable Option	**Objective**	**Action Needed**	**General Benefits**
Charitable Remainder Annuity Trust	Fixed income and potentially increases income.	Establish a charitable trust with property or other assets.	Immediate income tax deduction and fixed income for life.
Charitable Remainder Unittrust	Protect principal with varying income stream.	Establish a trust that pays a percentage of the trust's assets; income varies.	Immediate income tax deduction; annual income for life with potential increases.
Wealth Replacement Trust	Provide inheritance.	Use increased income or tax deduction to fund life insurance policy.	Heirs receive life insurance payout instead of property.
Charitable Lead Trust	Reduce gift and estate taxes on assets planned for heirs.	Create a trust that pays a fixed or variable income to charity for a set term, and then assets pass to heirs.	Reduced size of taxable estate; retains property in the family, often with reduced gift taxes.

Retained Life Estate	Gift personal residence with lifetime right of use.	Transfer title for home to charity, but retain occupancy.	Current income tax deduction with charity obtaining residence upon death.
Charitable Gift Annuity	Income with fixed annual payments from a contract rather than a trust.	Gift to charity in exchange for contractual payments.	Immediate and future savings on income taxes; fixed payments for life.
Pooled Income Fund	Improved income from low-rate-of-return property.	Commingle property or other assets with other donors.	Current income tax deduction; possible income improvement.